START-UP
GEOGRAPHY

RUBBISH AND RECYCLING

Anna Lee

Evans

Published by Evans Brothers Limited
2A Portman Mansions
Chiltern Street
London W1U 6NR

© Evans Brothers Limited 2003

Produced for Evans Brothers Limited by
White-Thomson Publishing Ltd.
2/3 St Andrew's Place
Lewes, East Sussex BN7 1UP

Printed in Hong Kong by Wing Ting Tong Co. Ltd.

Editor: Elaine Fuoco-Lang
Consultants: Lorraine Harrison, Senior Lecturer in
Geography Education at the University of Brighton
and Christine Bentall, Key Stage One teacher at
St Bartholomew's Church of England Primary
School, Brighton.
Designer: Tessa Barwick
Map artwork: The Map Studio

Cover: All photographs by Alan Towse

British Library Cataloguing in Publication Data
Lee, Anna
    Rubbish and recycling. - (Start-up geography)
    1.Recycling (Waste, etc.) - Juvenile literature
    I.Title
    363.7'282

ISBN: 0 237 52463 5

Acknowledgements:
The publishers would like to thank staff, students and
parents at Coldean Primary School, Brighton, for their
involvement in the preparation of this book.

Picture Acknowledgements:
All photographs by Alan Towse except Hodder Wayland
Picture Library 6, 18 *(left)*; Corbis 10 *(right)*;
Ecoscene/LNC HOSTEN 11 *(left)*; Ecoscene/Martin
Jones 12 *(bottom)*; Ecoscene/John Farmar 18 *(right)*;
Ecoscene/Wilkinson 19 *(left)*.

Contents

Our school

There are 150 pupils and 10 teachers at our school.
Every day all of us use things made of paper,
plastic or glass.

Sometimes we don't need them any more,
and they become rubbish.

paper   plastic   glass   rubbish

Rubbish can go in the bin
or be recycled ...

...but often it is
left lying around.

We call this rubbish 'litter'.

bin   recycled   litter

What happens to rubbish?

If we put our rubbish in a rubbish bin or a recycling container, the school caretaker collects it.

She puts it out for the rubbish truck, which takes rubbish to a waste disposal site.

recycling container   caretaker

Some rubbish is taken to the recycling plant.

Many things can be recycled.

What can you recycle at this plant?

waste disposal site   plant   7

Recycling

▶ **Recycling helps protect the environment.**

Recycling paper means that fewer trees are cut down to make new paper.

Recycling also means that less rubbish needs to be dumped.

protect environment trees

▲ At our school we recycle bottles, cans, newspapers and magazines.

Here are the different containers for each material.

Which container do the bottles go in?

And the cans?

bottles cans magazines

Problems with litter

Litter always looks unattractive.

Litter can spread germs ...

... and cause accidents.

unattractive germs accidents

It pollutes the water and can harm birds and fish.

Some litter ends up in rivers or the sea.

What do you think has happened to this bird?

pollutes   water   harm   rivers   sea

What creates rubbish?

Here are some places that are often quite dirty.

▶ What sort of rubbish collects outside a restaurant?

◀ Why is litter often found near ditches?

dirty   outside   near

▼ **There is very little rubbish in this park.**

Why do you think some places stay clean?

clean

Our Survey

We did a **survey** at school to find out where litter is found. To make it **fair**, we **counted** the number of pieces of litter at the same time every day for a week.

survey   fair   counted

This graph shows the results of the survey.

Which part of the playground is cleanest?

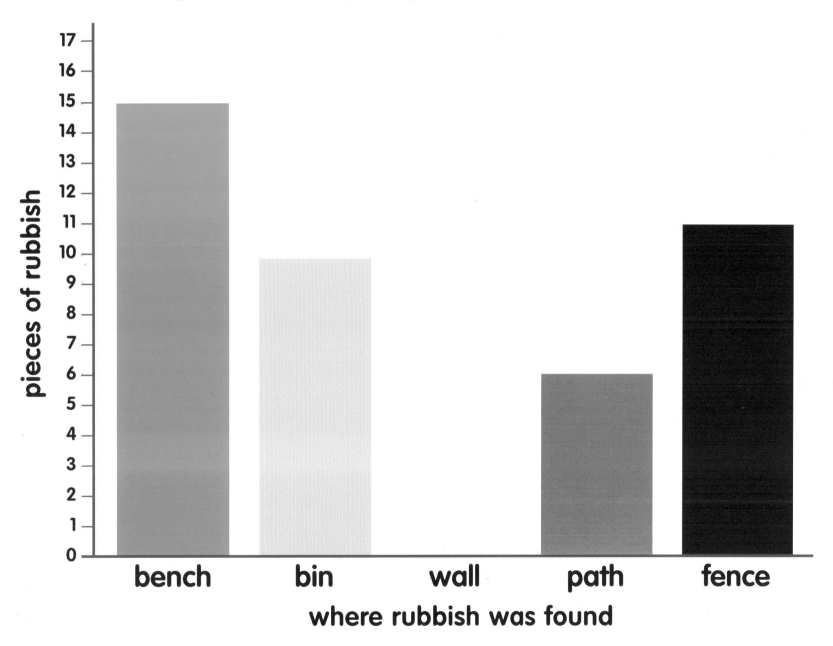

Improving the school environment

Our class decided to improve our school environment.

▶ We made signs asking everyone to clean up their own litter.

PLEASE PUT YOUR LITTER IN THE BIN OR RECYCLING CONTAINER.

No one should have to pick up other people's rubbish!

CANS ONLY

Southwark Council

CAN BANK

improve   signs

Finally, we wrote this letter to the local council asking for more recycling containers.

Coldean Primary School Selham Drive Coldean Brighton BN1 9EL
Headteacher: Mrs M Burdsey

tel: 01273 294914
fax: 01273 294916
e mail: office@coldean.brighton-hove.sch.uk

Dear Sir/Madam

We have been thinking about how we can improve our school environment. We already have some recycling containers at school, for paper, cans and bottles. We would like to be able to recycle plastic bottles as well. Please could you tell us if you could send us a container for recycling plastic?

Yours faithfully
Year two class
Coldean Primary School

What sort of containers did we ask for?

letter   local council

Improving the local area

These people are helping keep our **town** free of rubbish.

◀ Do you think this man should have to pick up other people's litter?

town

▶ We can help keep the **countryside** clean by taking our rubbish home.

◀ These boys are picking up litter in the countryside during a clean-up day.

countryside

Describing our

Here are some pictures of different places in our local area.

Use the words below to describe them.

clean, dirty, messy, tidy, dirtiest, cleanest, dirtier, cleaner, recycling, rubbish, litter.

local area

How could the dirty places be improved?

In what ways can we make less litter in the first place?

Further information for

New words listed in the text:

accidents	dirty	letter	plastic	sea
bin	environment	litter	pollutes	signs
bottles	fair	local council	protect	survey
cans	germs	magazines	recycled	town
caretaker	glass	near	recycling container	trees
clean	graph	outside	results	unattractive
counted	harm	paper	rivers	waste disposal site
countryside	improve	plant	rubbish	water

Possible Activities

SPREAD ONE

Discuss what the children use every day that is made of paper, plastic and glass. Discuss if these items are recycled at the school.

SPREAD TWO

Walk around the school and look at where bins or recycling containers are.

Invite a member of the council who deals with waste control into the school to discuss what happens to rubbish and recycling once it is collected.

SPREAD THREE

Conduct a survey to find out what is recycled at the school. Plot the results on a graph.

SPREAD FOUR

Discuss what accidents can happen when people drop rubbish. What effect does litter have on the environment?

Visit a local pond or stream and conduct a survey to see how much litter is present.

SPREAD FIVE

Take a walk around the local area and take photographs of places that are clean and places that are dirty. Stick the photographs to a map of the local area. Discuss which areas are the cleanest and which are the dirtiest.

Write a letter to the local council asking if the local area can be made cleaner and safer.

Parents and Teachers

SPREAD SIX

Conduct your own school survey to see what litter is dropped at different places around the school.

Make a sign to show children where the rubbish and recycling bins are in areas where the most litter is dropped.

Set up a litter patrol to discover what times of day the most litter is dropped. Different groups could survey the playground in the morning, at playtime, before and after lunch and at the end of the day.

Plot a graph to show at what time of the day the most litter is dropped.

SPREAD SEVEN

Make a poster to ask people to recycle and put them on a noticeboard.

Write a letter to the local council asking what other things the school can do to help with recycling.

SPREAD EIGHT

Discuss what could be done to improve the appearance of the local area. Have any improvements been made to the local area in recent years? Discuss what these are.

SPREAD NINE

Take photographs of places in the local area. What words would you use to describe these places?

Stick the photographs to a map of the local area and ask children to say which place is their favourite. Plot a graph to show the most and least favourite place in the local area.

Further Information

BOOKS

FOR CHILDREN

Places We Share by Sally Hewitt (Franklin Watts 2000)
Shopping by Sally Hewitt (Franklin Watts 2000)
Street by Sally Hewitt (Franklin Watts 2000)
Where We Live by Sally Hewitt (Franklin Watts 2000)
The Street by Jeff Stanfield (Hodder Wayland 1999)

FOR ADULTS

Handbook of Primary Geography by Roger Carter (Ed) (The Geographical Association 1998)
Also contact your local council

WEBSITES

http://www.standards.dfee.gov.uk/schemes/geography
http://www.learn.co.uk
http://www.schoolzone.co.uk

Index